This WORKBook belongs to an incredible CReaToR of DReaMS Come true...

Name:

Contact Details:

DRaw oR Add a photo of You

DEDICATION

to DAWSY + ouR
2 meRMAiDS + ouR
PROMiSE to CREATE
an Amazing life
together ♥♥♥

PhilanthROPY
is ♥
in Action

A PoRtion of
PROfits fRoM EVERY
book is RE-DiRected
to AUSTRALIAN
WILDLiFE CONSERVANCY

Book
Deets

©Leonie Dawson
International PtY LtD
SEND feedback to:
SUPPoRT @
LEONIEDAWSON.COM

HeY. ThANK You
foR BEiNG BoRN ♥
ThANK You foR Being
You! ♥ Me

CONTENTS!

MUST HAVE ITEM

"I've been using the workbooks for a few years now. They've allowed me to achieve some really crazy goals I've set for myself. They are a must-have if you want to create an amazing year."

- **Denise Duffield-Thomas, author of** *"Lucky Bitch"*

A GUIDE TO BUILD MY BUSINESS

"Leonie Dawson's workbooks are SO powerful. I have used them every year for the last 8 years. I gush about them all the time. Whatever I put in these workbooks ends up becoming destiny. I cannot recommend them enough"

-**Hibiscus Moon, author + crystal expert**

HIGHLY RECOMMENDED

"I love these workbooks and have used them for years for my life and business. Whatever I write in there ends up happening. I highly recommend them."

- **Nathalie Lussier, entrepreneur, AccessAlly**

TRULY TOOK MY BUSINESS TO THE NEXT LEVEL!

"[This] workbook was the swift kick in the butt I needed to start looking at my business for what it really is— a huge source of joy in my life. Since doing the workbook I have tripled my monthly income and found financial freedom in my business!"

- Flora Sage, author, speaker + coach

HELPED ME CREATE AN AUTHENTIC BUSINESS!

"[This] workbook helped me identify what really mattered to me in my business and life, and helped me develop a business that was completely grounded in those values."

- Katie Cowan, Symphony Law's founder

I CANNOT TELL YOU THE IMPACT THAT THE WORKBOOK HAD ON MY BUSINESS!

"Leonie's straight talking, comprehensible approach to business made it easy for me to take all the steps I had either been avoiding or wasn't even aware I should be taking. Within a month I had not only been brave enough to set income targets for the first time, I had met and overshot them!"

- Kate Beddow, holistic therapist

EASY & POWERFUL WAY TO TRANSFORM!

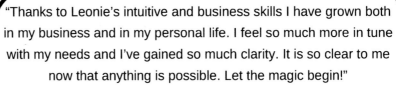

"Thanks to Leonie's intuitive and business skills I have grown both in my business and in my personal life. I feel so much more in tune with my needs and I've gained so much clarity. It is so clear to me now that anything is possible. Let the magic begin!"

- Karina Ladet, intuitive healer

AMAZED AT THE IMPACT IT HAD! "Wow! I'm a big forward thinker and straight away this shifted my thinking because first up I had to reflect on the year just past which was incredibly powerful. . . I ended up purchasing copies for several of my coaching clients so they could enjoy the experience of completing their own workbook too!"

- Belinda Jackson, business strategist

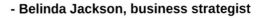

I WAS BLOWN AWAY!

"To be honest, I was a bit skeptical when I bought the workbook. However, I was BLOWN AWAY by the value offered. After going through the workbooks, I had a clear plan for achieving both my personal and business goals. I'm now calmer, more focused, and more productive. My monthly income has more than doubled!"

- Shay de Silva, fitness coach + founder of Fast Fitness To Go

The New Year stands before us, like a chapter in a book waiting to be written. we can help WRITE THAT STORY by setting goals.

-Melody Beattie

CONGRATULATIONS

on choosing to go on the GREAT GRAND adventure that is GOAL setting. THIS RIGHT HERE ⊙ in this very moment, your life is changing. YOU are a CONSCIOUS CREATOR of your own Life. YOU are a BIRTHER of DREAMS and the CAPTAIN of YOUR OWN Adventure.

This WORKBOOK will be YOUR

companion   dREAM Midwife   cheerleader

👁 can't WAIT to see what you CREATE with it ♥♥♥

? What do you need to do to make that shift happen?

Step 1: Take the vow

I, _____
NAME

do solemnly swear that I am committed to my own success. That I am 100% Responsible for my actions + subsequent results. By aligning my actions with my intentions, I become a Powerful Creator of My Own Destiny.

_____ SIGNED _____ DATE

②. Fill out this workbook

It is NOT ENOUGH to just BUY it & use it as a paper-weight.

You must actually **DO THE THING & FILL IT OUT!**

③. SET A DEADLINE

JAN
30

Decide **NOW** when you will have this workbook Completed by ↱

I commit to finishing this workbook by:

_____
DATE

_____
SIGNED

④ Schedule in Your Goals

Once You've set goals:

Take a look at YouR YeaRLY calendaR. MaP out some of when YouR Big goals could happen.

Look at YouR daily + weekly schedule to Build in Goal Getting time!

⑤ Surround YOUrSELF with other GOAL-GETTERS

gift this Book To fRieNds!

Start A WoRKBook GRouP!

join MY WoRKBook Facebook group!

> "You aRe the AveRage OF the 5 PeoPle You SPeNd YouR time witH. Make them good ONeS!"
> —JIM ROHN

6. Regularly Look at Your Goals!

The more you remember & review your goals, the faster they will come true! It will help you align your daily habits in the direction of your dreams.

Carry this book with you until it is dog-eared & well loved ♥

Create a desktop wallpaper that reminds you of your goals

Keep a note on you with your Top 3 Goals you are working on ★

Use the monthly check-in worksheets in this book!

A **Millionaire** LOOKS AT THEIR GOALS **ONCE** A DAY.

A **Billionaire** LOOKS AT THEIR GOALS **TWICE** A DAY.

Want to be in the top (1%) of achievers?

80% of PEOPLE DON'T EVEN THINK of GOALS

16% THINK OF GOALS BUT DON'T write them down

3% write down their goals but never look at them again

JUST 1% WRITE DOWN their goals AND REGULARLY REVIEW THEM. THESE PEOPLE ARE AMONG THE ☆ highest Achievers ☆

Why LEARN from LEONIE?

- ♥ Internationally best-selling author
- ♥ Has created over $14 Million in Revenue in 10 hours a week
- ♥ WINNER of AusMumpreneur's Businesses Making A Difference Award Global Brand AWARD & People's Choice Business Coach Award
- ♥ CREATOR of the BRilliant Biz + Life academy ★

DO YOU NEED to fill out this whole book for it to work ?

YES

Something is better than NOTHING!
Do what you can or are called to.
The MORE you put in, the MORE You will
get out of it. ♥ Your Future
SELF Will thank You ♥

RESULTS You can get from using the workbooks

MORE **DREAMS** & GOALS ACHIEVED

INCREASED **Self** CONFIDENCE

A circle of WONDERFUL INSPIRING **GOAL-Getter FRIENDS**

DE♥EPER, MORE FULFILLING RELATION-SHIPS

PURPOSE, DIRECTION & **MOTIVATION**

IMPROVED PRODUCTIVITY

A WILD SURGE of **JOYFUL CREATIVITY**

YOUR BUCKET LIST BEING TICKED OFF!

SKY HIGH LEVELS OF **JOY, LOVE, CALM &** FULFILLMENT

INSIDE YOU THERE
is the (🌱 Seed) of a
Great Tree,
far   LARGER
& (more) MaGNiF
              -icent
than   YOU can
POS   SIBLY
                   SEE
RiGHt   NOW.

Let's Review the PAST YEAR

WHY REVIEW
the Past Year?

So often we want to →JUMP straight into setting NEW goals, dreaming NEW DREAMS before we do the

ALL IMPORTANT WORK

of reviewing the Past Year.

To leap FORWARD into the future, we must first:

1. KNOW where we are Right Now

2. Take the time to Mine for clarity insights Lessons from the Past Year. It is a veritable treasure chest of GOLDEN WISDOM just waiting for You! ♥

Last Year's Review

BEST DAY:

WORST DAY:

Momentous Events:

BIRTHS CELEBRATED:

DEATHS GRIEVED:

MOST EXCITING thiNG:

Scariest thing that happened:

PLACES VISITED:

YOU ARE MAGIC

WHO or WHAT inspired you?

WHO did you inspire?

What new things did you try?

WHO did you get to KNOW MORE?

where did you spend your time?

WHAT was the KINDEST thing you said to someone?

What was the KINDEST thing someone said to you?

What made you **happy?**

What **WORRIED** you most?

QUOTE OF THE YEAR:

A POLITICAL OR **WORLD** EVENT that AFFECTED YOU:

♡ SOMETHING YOU **REGRET** DOING...

♡ SOMETHING YOU **WISH** YOU HAD DONE...

BEST EVENT:

✐ FAVOURITE THING YOU **MADE:**

favourite
people

BEST
movie
WATCHED

Music
YOU PLAYED
ON Repeat

TV shows
YOU
BINGED ON

favourite
drink

FAVOURITE
Meal

BEST
hug

favourite
outfit

favourite
gift
received

favourite
gift
GIVEN

BEST Books Read

1.

2.

3.

4.

5.

6.

7.

8.

9.

10.

Let's PLAY
EVERYBODY'S
faVouRite
game Show

↓

WHAT WORKED?
WHAT DIDN'T?

WHAT WORKED?

WHAT DIDN'T?

TRAVEL and ADVENTURES

FAMILY and FRIENDSHIPS

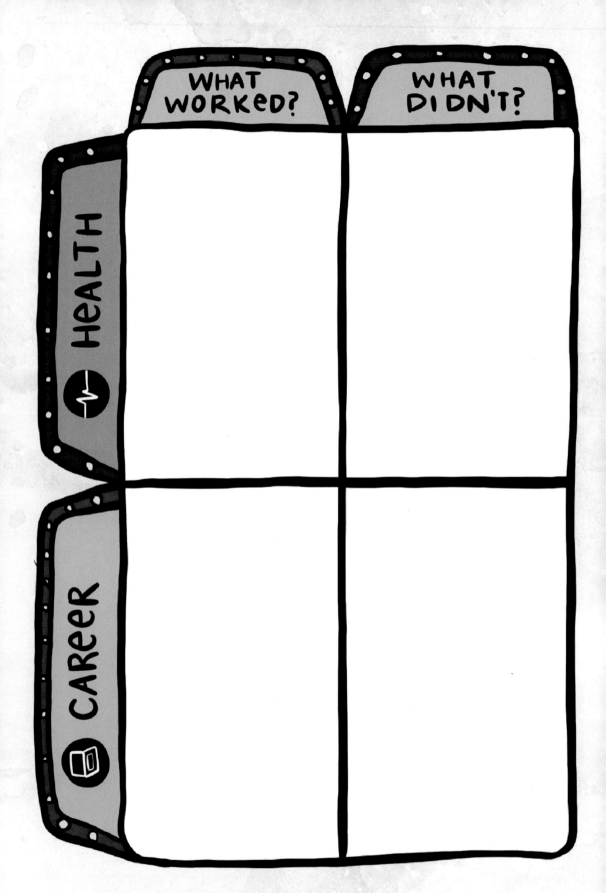

WHAT WORKED?

WHAT DIDN'T?

HEALTH

CAREER

	WHAT WORKED?	**WHAT DIDN'T?**
CREATIVITY		
SELF CARE & MENTAL HEALTH		

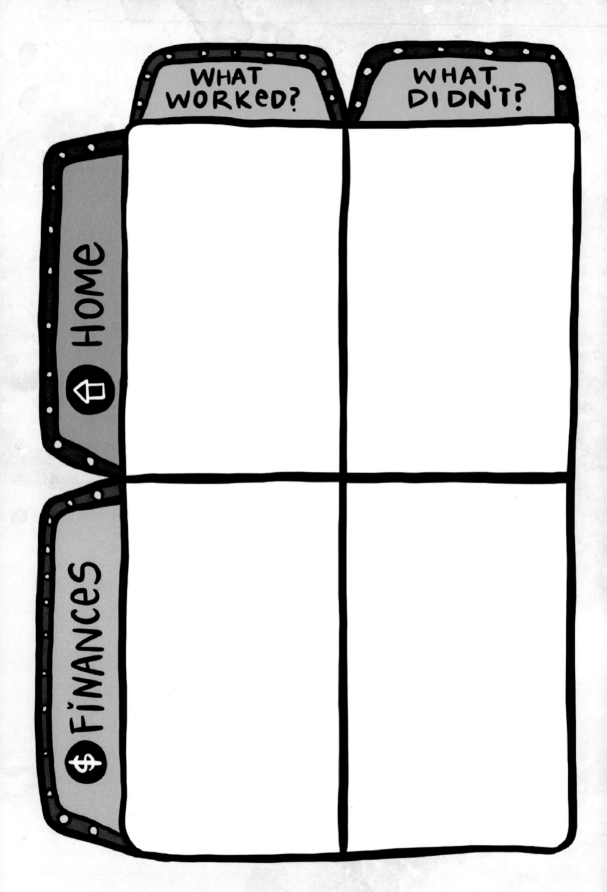

WHAT WORKED?

WHAT DIDN'T?

HOME

FINANCES

WE can DO HARD ThinGS.

GLennoN DoYLE

What were the biggest **BLESSINGS** of the Year?

What were the biggest **CHALLENGES?**

What DID YOU **LEARN** over the last YEAR?

What are You **PROUD** of YOURSELF foR?

what AREAS of YOUR life felt OUT of WHACK OR CRAZY-MAKING over the last YEAR?

what could BE OR fix DONE to change these AREAS?

What do you need to WRITE, JOURNAL or RANT about to feel clear about your life from the last YEAR?

A PAGE for GRATITUDE

DRAW, WRITE, illustrate OR ADD photos of EVERYTHING YOU ARE grateful foR IN YouR life from the past YeaR...

COMPLETION CIRCLE

I breathe & give thanks for all that HAS PASSED.

I OPEN UP to ALL the beautiful possibilities BLOSSOMING before me.

I Let go & breathe. Releasing all that holds me back FROM MY Magnificence.

I AM safe. I AM LOVED. I AM KNOWN. I have 1000 angels cheering me on.

Place your hand in the circle.

invoking the year ahead

It's time to DREAM a NEW DREAM. It's time to create a Brilliant, Shining Year for You + Your WORLD. First comes the THOUGHT, then comes the WORD, then the ACTION. Are You READY? ☐ YES ☐ NO

CREATE a VISION that MAKES YOU want to JUMP out of Bed in the Morning!

InVoKing - - - - - - - - -

This year I want to feel:

This year I want to let go of:

This year I want to give myself the gift of:

This year I promise to myself that:

This will be the year that...

MY Creative GOALS

WHAT ARE YOUR CREATIVE GOALS FOR THIS YEAR?

which goal out of these is your most important creative goal?

_____

_____

What's a creative project you haven't done since you were a kid?

what makes you feel CREATIVELY INSPIRED?

_____
_____
_____
_____
_____

what CREATIVE PROJECT would you DO if you weren't afraid?

_____
_____
_____
_____

How could you foster your own CREATIVE Community?

_____
_____
_____
_____

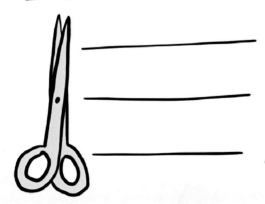

OUR **ART**
MUST BE made
OUR Stories
MUST BE told
OUR GIFtS
MUST BE shared

CREATIVE POSSIBILITIES!

Circle what you'd like to try this coming year...

Photography

WRITE A SONG

Learn GUITAR

MAKE BIG ART

NEEDLE FELTING

LEARN OIL PAINTING

Write A BOOK

Paper making

MAKE Candles

WOOD WORK

POTTERY

TiE DYE

JEWELRY MAKING

Ultimate CUPCAKE BAKING

SCRAP booking

Sculpture

Sing (OR JOIN A CHOIR)

LeaRN a MUSiCaL iNStRuMeNt

MaKe a NatuRe MoBiLe

SeND HaND WRitten LetteRS

Start a PODCAST

Make A Stained glass window

MaKe A MOVie

Keep A PinteRest BoaRD of PoSSible projects & DO THEM!

TRY A NeW MeDiUM

- ☐ WaTeRcoLouR
- ☐ Gouache
- ☐ ACRYLic
- ☐ Oil
- ☐ Pastels
- ☐ CharcoaL
- ☐ Sketching
- ☐ PoRtRait
- ☐ Landscape
- ☐ Hyper Realism
- ☐ Abstract
- ☐ Cartooning
- ☐ Sculpture

Take A Creative Course (online or IRL!)

KNitting

Make a KiTchen window heRB garden

Learn to sew

Make heRbal or essential oil Potions

WRite A BOOK IN 40 DAYS

Want HeLP? Take MY e-course
LEONiEDAWSON.COM/BOOK

RECOMMENDED RESOURCES FOR **CReAtivity**

THE ARTIST'S WAY · JULIA CAMERON

& EVERYthing else she's ever ever ever written

MAKING COMICS · LYNDA BARRY

A CReAtive COMPANION · SARK

BIG MAGIC · Elizabeth Gilbert

THE CREATIVE LICENCE · D. Gregory

LIVING OUT LOUD · Keri Smith

All of AUSTIN KLEON's BOOKs

BIRD BY BIRD · Anne Lamott

The Creative Habit · T. THARP

Letters to A YOUNG POET · R.M. Rilke

How To MAKE A JOURNAL OF YOUR LIFE · D. Price

LUCY Knisley's graphic Memoirs

MY "FINISH YOUR BOOK in 40 DAYS" COURSE!

Clear Mind, Wild Heart · David Whyte

Most of all... don't just **READ** about creating... CREATE! Do the thing!

47

You have permission to make your own world that is the truest painting of YOU!

MY CAREER & EDUCATION GOALS

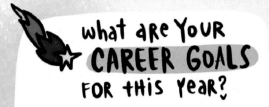 what are YOUR **CAREER GOALS** FOR this year?

what would YOU like to DO **Differently** in YOUR career this year?

 DO YOU NEED to **NETWORK?** if yes, how?

what **SKILLS** do YOU NEED to DEVELOP?

What **TEACHERS** & **MENTORS** do you need?

What **COURSES** & **CONFERENCES** would you like to invest in?

What **BOOKS** do you want to **READ?**

YOU were

born

to be →

YOU

for a VeRy

important

reason

MY
Family & Friendship
GOALS

 My FAMILY & FRIENDSHIP Goals for this YeaR...

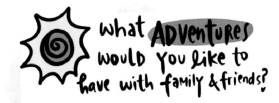 What ADVENTURES would you like to have with family & friends?

L Family & friends id ♥ to Spend time with this year...

! New friendships & Relationships id like to create would look like this:

ways I'd like to **DEEPEN** my friendships & relationships:

ways I could MAKE my **FAMILY LIFE** calmer & less CRAZY this YEAR:

& if you are a PaRent...

How can I help MY children **thrive** this YeaR?

what do I need to **thRive** as a PaRent this YeaR?

RECOMMENDED RESOURCES FOR *family & friendships*

What we say matters ♥ I & J Lasater

I Need Your Love - IS That TRUE? ♥ Byron Katie

TINY Beautiful Things ♥ Cheryl Strayed

MOMMA ZEN ♥ Karen Maezen Miller

GOOD MOTHER WELCOME ♥ I. GOFF-MAIDOFF

ALL books BY Steve BiDDulph

THE GIFTS OF IMPERFECT PARENTING Brené Brown

The RAINBOW WAY ♥ LucY PEARCE

REAL talk here... Books are great but Relationship & family counsellors are even better... IF YOUR CAR was broken, You'd take it to a Mechanic. If YOUR Relationships need REPAIR, GO to a PROFESSional!

carry on, WARRIOR ♥ GLENNON DOYLE

5 LOVE LANGUAGES . gary chapman

MY health GOALS

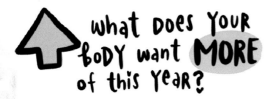 WHAT DOES YOUR BODY want MORE of this YEAR?

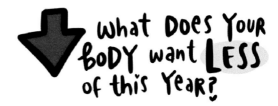 WHAT DOES YOUR BODY want LESS of this YEAR?

WHAT KINDS OF ACTIVITIES will MAKE YOUR BODY Shine this YEAR?

WHAT KIND OF FOOD will MAKE YOUR bodY Shine this YEAR?

HOW MY BODY feels RIGHT NOW...

COLOUR IN, COLLAGE, draw it out...

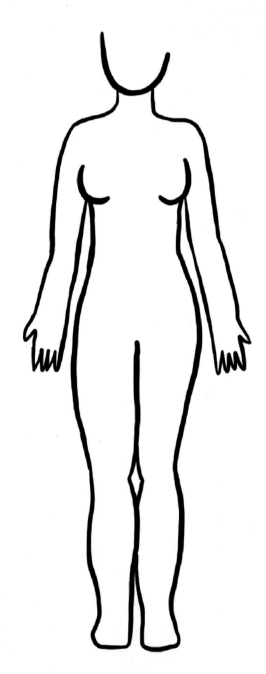

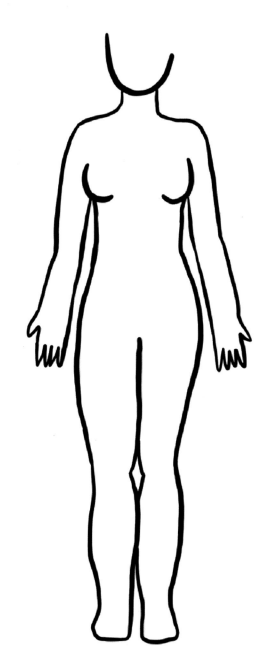

HOW I WANT MY BODY to feel this YEAR...

COLOUR IN,
COLLAGE,
DRAW it out...

MOVEMENT OPTIONS

CIRCLE what YOU want to TRY this YEAR...

RUNNING

HIKING

ice skating

SURFING

Swimming

BICYCLING!

hula hooping

KAYAKING

SAILING

CHOOSE YOUR TYPE of DANCE →

- ♥ Ballroom
- ♥ Line DANCING
- ♥ SALSA
- ♥ ecstatic DANCE
- ♥ ZUMBA ♥ NiA ♥ Jive
- ♥ Belly Dancing
- ♥ 5Rhythms
- ♥ LOUNGEROOM crazy dancing

WALK ON beach

YOGA

aqua aerobics

GOLF

MINI GOLF

pilates

DISCO Rollerskating

CIRCUS classes

ROCK CLIMB ING

TRAMPO-lining

PING PONG

EXTREME FRISBEE

WEIGHT lifting

ADD YOUR OWN HERE

👁 make
my own
dreams
come true.

MY home GOALS

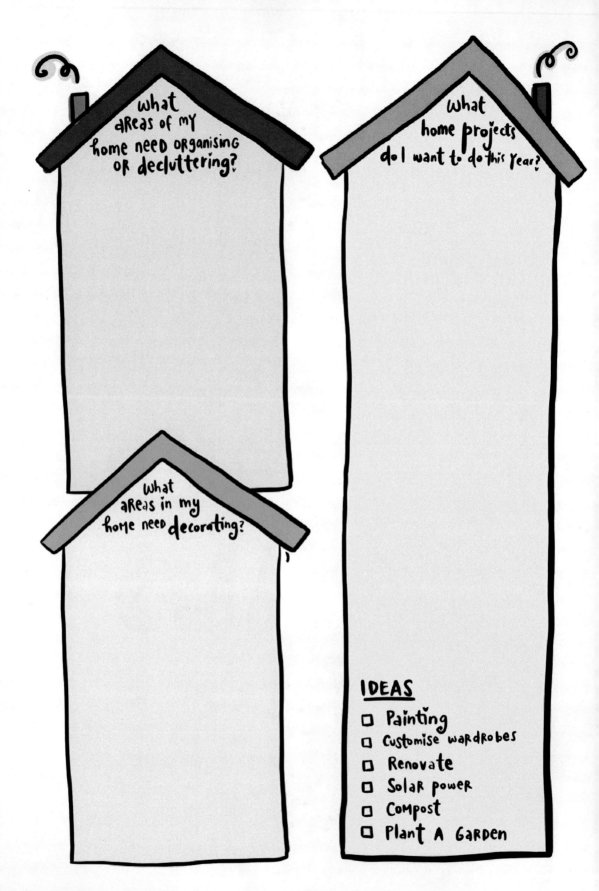

What areas of my home need organising or decluttering?

What home projects do I want to do this year?

What areas in my home need decorating?

IDEAS

- ☐ Painting
- ☐ Customise wardrobes
- ☐ Renovate
- ☐ Solar power
- ☐ Compost
- ☐ Plant a garden

How Do I want my house to **feel** this yeaR?

What aRe some things I could Do to make it feel like that?

Do I have a SPACE of MY OWN to cReate, Rest, Reflect & be with MySELF?

YES

NO

If No, can I cReate one?

If Yes, how can I impRove it?

YOUR
glorious
LIFE IS
→ RIGHT HERE ←
READY to BE

chosen.

MY travel & adventure GOALS

Places Id love to visit this Year:

People id love to visit this YeaR:

ADMIT ONE

what's a MOVIE, CONCERT OR
SHOW YOU'D love to see this YEAR?

ADMIT ONE

what EVENTS OR ATTRACTIONS
would you love to go to this YEAR?

COLOUR in where You'd like to travel to 🡒

I am a **Devotee** of my **Dreams** & a **goddess** of my **goals**

MY Money GOALS

MONEY REVIEW

 KnowleDge is POWER & CLARITY. To Start growing our $MONEY, we NEED to See where we have already BEEN.

How Much MONEY did You RECEIVE last YEAR?	
How Much MONEY did You SAVE last Year?	

Make a Pie Chart of how you SPENT YOUR Money Last Year

 Make a Pie Chart of how You WANT to Spend YOUR Money this YEAR

How much MONEY would you like to RECEIVE this year?

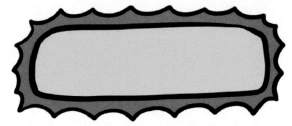

How much MONEY would you like to SAVE this year?

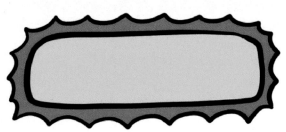

How do you want to INVEST YOUR Money this YEAR?

(OR even just LEARN moRE ABout!)

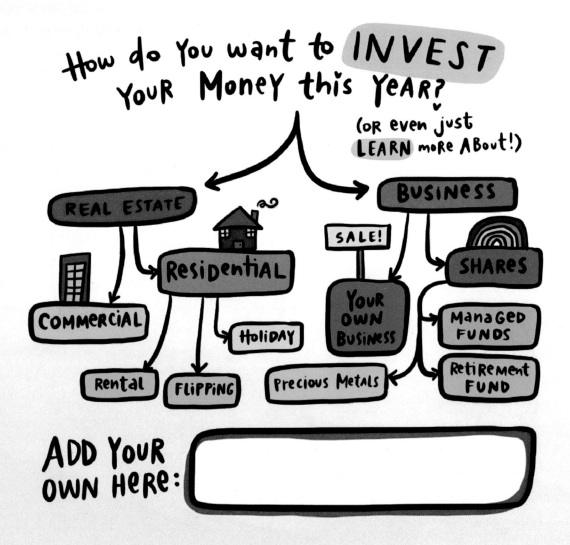

REAL ESTATE

Residential

COMMERCIAL

Holiday

Rental

FLIPPING

SALE!

YOUR OWN Business

Precious Metals

BUSiNESS

SHARES

ManaGED FUNDS

RETiREMENT FUND

ADD YOUR OWN HERE:

What can you do to INCREASE YOUR income this YEAR?

What can you do to REDUCE YOUR expenses this YEAR?

YOU CAN DO this!

WAYS TO BECOME a GREAT MONEY CUSTODIAN

CIRCLE how you want to develop your fiscal powers this year...

 Pay off all **DEBT**

 Read A **MONEY** book

 INVEST IN **STOCKS**, index funds or managed funds

 Learn about **REAL estate**

 Make a **BUDGET**

 **TRACK YOUR MONEY**

 Find a great **BOOK KEEPER + accountant**

 TRY an online money management system (like MINT.com or YNAB.com)

 Find + consolidate super/retirement accounts

 **WORK on YOUR money blocks**

 Add **YOUR OWN**

 Research **FINANCIAL Independence Retire Early** books + blogs

Calculate YOUR Personal NET WORTH

Oh how fun! Let's look at your current net worth. Remember this is not an indication of your soul's worth. And your current net worth is just a baseline you can GROW 🌱

ASSETS (what you own)	$ WORTH
Car	
House	
Super/retirement savings	
Shares	
Cash	
Business	
TOTAL ASSETS	$

LIABILITIES (what you owe)	$ COST
Credit card debt	
Mortgage	
Loans	
Total Liabilities	$

NET WORTH (Assets minus liabilities)	

To Make Your dreams come true, Align Your ACTiONS WITH YOUR iNTENTIONS.

MY
change
the World
GOALS

How would you *like* the **WORLD** to change this YEAR?

What can **YOU** do to help make that change?

HOW MUCH **MONEY** WOULD YOU LIKE TO DONATE THIS YEAR?

To which CAUSES?

How will you donate your **time & ENERGY** this year?

How do you want to DO BETTER?

Have a No Buy Month. OR Say NO to fast fashion.

PLANT TREES

START COMPOSTING

COOK FOR A FAMILY OR OLDER PERSON WHO NEEDS IT

KIVA.ORG
Make a loan to someone

PICK UP RUBBISH

REDUCE YOUR Plastic WASTE

COMMIT to LEARNING & BEING ANTI-RACIST

Move to ethical & SUSTAINABLE investment funds & SUPERANNUATION

Become A CLIMATE CRISIS Activist

SPONSOR AN ANIMAL

BUY & EAT locally & independently

CHOOSE MORE ORGANIC

GROW YOUR OWN garden (OR EVEN just A Kitchen HERB POT!)

Anti- RACIST
RECOMMENDED READING!

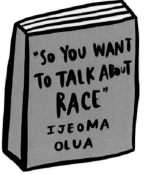

"SO YOU WANT TO TALK ABOUT RACE" IJEOMA OLUA

"TALKING TO MY COUNTRY" STAN GRANT

GOOD TALK — MIRA JACOBS

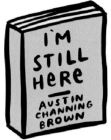

I'M STILL HERE — AUSTIN CHANNING BROWN

WHITE SPACES MISSING FACES — C. Jackson

DARK EMU — Bruce Pascoe

THIS WILL BE MY UNDOING — MORGAN JENKINS

WHY I'M NO LONGER TALKING TO WHITE PEOPLE ABOUT RACE — RENI EDDO-LODGE

YOUR BLACK FRIEND — B. PASSMORE

FOR MORE anti-Racist EDUCATION RESOURCES GO TO www.LEONIEDAWSON.COM/RACISM

Change The World
RECOMMENDED READING!

WILDING
isabella
TREE

CREATING
ROOM
TO
READ
J. WOODS

THIS IS
NOT A
DRILL
EXTINCTION
REBELLION

CHAPTER
ONE
Daniel
FlYNN

DARE
TO
LEAD
B. Brown

EVERY WOMAN's
GUIDE TO
SAVING
THE PLANET
NATALIE
ISAACS

THE YEAR
OF LESS
CAIT
FLANDERS

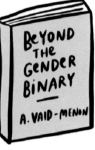
BEYOND
THE
GENDER
BINARY
A. VAID-MENON

EL
DEAFO
CE CE
BELL

GENDER
QUEER
MAIA
KOBABE

QUEER
M.J. Barker
&
J. Scheele

QUICK + EASY
GUIDE To
THEY/
THEM
PRONOUNS
A. Bonjiovanni
T. JIMERSON

QUICK + EASY
GUIDE To
QUEER +
TRANS
IDENTITIES
MADY G.
J.R. Zuckerberg

MORE gender, SexUALITY, DiSABILITY &
TRANS READING at LEONIEDAWSON.COM/GENDER

This world can CHANGE & we are the ONES WHO WILL CHANGE it.

MY Self Care & Mental Health GOALS

why do we need BOUNDARIES?

> "You have the Right to say "NO" without feeling guilty." - MANUEL J. SMITH

> " when we FAIL to set BOUNDARIES & hold PEOPLE ACCOUNTABLE, we feel USED & MISTREATED." - Brené BROWN

what BOUNDARIES do you need to CREATE & UPHOLD this YEAR?

_____

_____

_____

_____

_____

_____

_____

What are YOU Going to STOP doing this YeaR in YOUR LiFe?

If You want to start creating NEW things, a NEW energy, expansion OR era for Yourself, You need to clear out the oLD.

You need to get Rid of old:

HABits   Projects   Patterns   Beliefs

OBligations   Lifestyle choices

that aren't helping you move forward. Add what You will STOP doing BELOW...

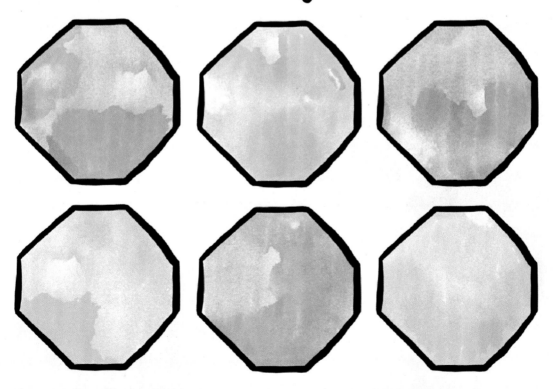

RETREAT

It can be incredibly nourishing, inspiring + soul-affirming to take time away to fill your own cup – especially if you are a parent or carer. Even taking just one night away can ≥illuminate≤ your whole year!

WHEN?

WHERE?

HOW LONG?

What will you do?

NOW schedule it in! Put it in your calendar! Make it happen!

Ritual DaYS

We all need to do things that fill us up... it's just hard to remember to fit it in sometimes... Here's where RITUAL DAYS come in handy! What are all the things you want to do weekly? Turn them into days!

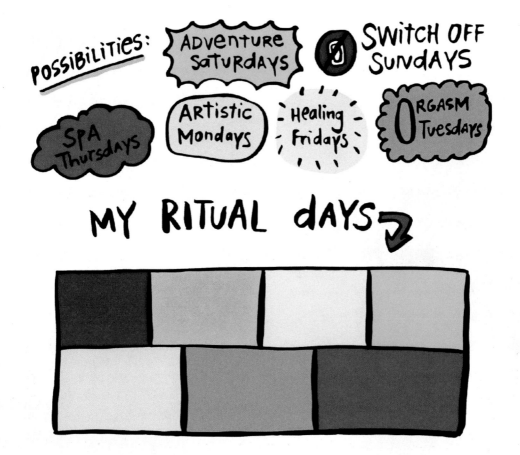

POSSIBILITIES:
- ADVENTURE SaturDAYS
- SWITCH OFF SundAYS
- SPA Thursdays
- ARTistic Mondays
- Healing Fridays
- ORGASM Tuesdays

MY RITUAL DAYS

This year I give myself permission to...

Write yourself some permission slips!

I HEREBY GIVE PERMISSION TO:

_____
YOUR NAME HERE

TO: _____   SIGNED
                                          The Universe

_____

I HEREBY GIVE PERMISSION TO:

_____
YOUR NAME HERE

TO: _____   SIGNED
                                          The Universe

_____

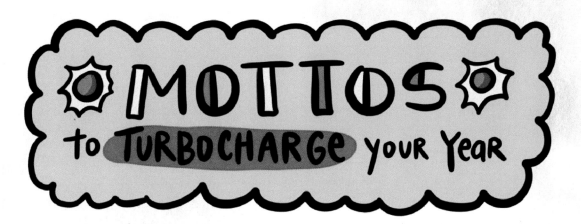

MOTTOS

to TURBOCHARGE your Year

For an easy way to remember what you are wishing to cultivate, create gorgeous mottos to live by. Here's some examples of mottos for making a magnificent year:

JOY is an OPTION

LOVE MORE. ♥ onwards

We can do HARD THINGS

Say YES!

go slower do less

CULTIVATE MAGIC

things 👁 want to celebrate about myself

POP A Photo OR draw a Picture of YOURSELF in the flower's centre. Then add YOUR CELEBrations in the Petals!

SURROUNDED BY LOVE

Paste a PHOTO of YOURSELF in the heart frame. Then surround yourself with LOVE LETTERS, Reminders, messages of support -all the things you need to hear right now ♥✓

Support Menu

What Kind Of Support Do You Want?

- ☑ Child Care
- ☑ Therapist
- ☐ Massage
- ☐ Closer friendship Circle
- ☐ Women's Circle
- ☐ Financial education
- ☑ Intuitive healing
- ☑ Stylist
- ☑ Cleaner
- ☐ Accountability
- ☐ Life coach
- ☐ Personal Trainer
- ☐ Quiet Time
- ☑ Gardener
- ☑ More Social Fun!

DREAM UP YOUR OWN SUPPORT ↺ POSSIBILITIES HERE ↴

- ☑ - - - - - - - - - -
- ☐ - - - - - - - - - -
- ☑ - - - - - - - - - -
- ☐ - - - - - - - - - -

How would you like to CELEBRATE your BIRTHDAY this year?

Do you have enough SUPPORT in your LIFE to thrive this year?

YES ◼   NO ◼

If you were fully SUPPORTED in every area of your LIFE, what would that LOOK LIKE?

AFFIRMATIONS

Create your own. Collage. Cut out.
Put around your home, in your diary + pockets.

CREATE AN Everyday Miracles Jar

EVERYDAY Miracles

get a large JAR, TUB or BOX.

You can DECORATE it beautifully if you want. PAINT, Collage, MOD PODGE, gLitter.

WRITE DOWN

YOUR everyday Miracles as they happen on small pieces of paper.

Ceremoniously

PLACE them in YOUR EVERYDAY MIRACLES JAR while humming "EYE of the TIGER" (that or just fold & pop them in)

What Kinds of Everyday Miracles Should I Write?

unexpected Letters & parcels

random ACTS OF KINDNESS

The most DELICIOUS MEAL OR PERFECT cup of TEA

Sweet Moments OR Dear CONNECTIONS

The Moment you laugh so hard you nearly wet your pants!

AT THE END OF ♥ THE YEAR ♥

You will have a precious collection to REFLECT ON, celebrate & START YOUR New Year feeling gratitude!

CUT OUT + use as a label for the JAR

A JAR FOR COLLECTING everyday Miracles

What To Do When EVERYTHING SUCKS

There's going to be hard moments in the year ahead. We can prep for them by brainstorming what helps us shift our mood. Our feelings can change in a moment. Fickle things they are - generated by our environment, body, situation & perspective. Let's brainstorm what gentle changes can help you shift the mood when everything sucks!

LEONIE'S LIST OF DESUCKIFICATION
- ♥ Go outside
- ♥ Smell lavender
- ♥ Eat something green ♥
- ♥ Have a shower
- ♥ Do 10 mins of stretching

CUT OUT + PUT IN A HANDY PLACE (YOUR PURSE OR PHONE) FOR A SUCKTASTIC EMERGENCY

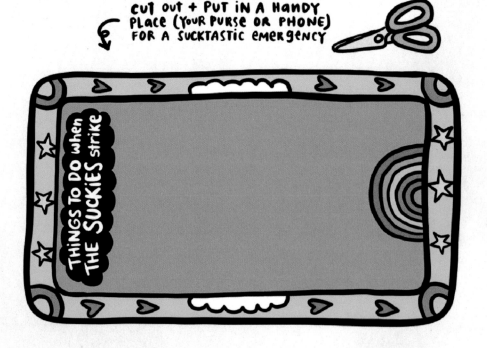

THINGS TO DO when THE SUCKIES strike

RECOMMENDED RESOURCES FOR
Self Care & Mental Health

THE ART OF EXTREME SELF CARE — CHERYL RichardSON

THE WOMAN'S COMFORT BOOK — Jennifer LOUDEN

Transformation SOUP — SARK

HOW TO BE A WOMAN — CAITLYN MORAN

FIRST, WE Make THE BEAST BEAUTIFUL — S. WiLSON

ROCK STEADY — ELLEN FORNEY

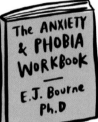
The ANXIETY & PHOBIA WORKBOOK — E.J. Bourne Ph.D

MORE THAN A WOMAN — CaitLiN MORAN

SELF COMPASSION — KRiSten NEFF

GiFTS OF IMPERFECTION — Brené BROWN

THRiVE — ARIANNA HuFFiNGToN

BOOKS BY SuSan Branch

Want to READ my WRITINGS about my DEPRESSION + ANXIETY?
LEONIEDAWSON.COM/MYANXIETY

WE CAN DO HARD THINGS
PODCAST

Rounding it all UP!

Time Review

Pie Chart of
HOW YOU
CURRENTLY SPEND
YOUR TIME

HOW YOU
want to
spend
YOUR
TIME

MY GOAL Getter habits

WHAT joyful & NOURISHING HABITS WOULD YOU LIKE to cultivate OVER the Next YEAR? Don't worry aBout HOW HARD IT IS to FORM HABITS - WHAT we'll BE DOING instead is CREATING A POSTER to REMIND ourselves each DAY OF THE Beautiful THINGS WE'D ♥ To Do!

SOME DAYS WE Might Do all of them, MOST DAYS We'll ONLY GET To SOME... OTHER DAYS WE MAY Not Get to ANY.

all of this is gorgeous & fine ♥

It's Not ABout PERFECTION OR FAILURE. It's ABout REMINDING ourselves OF the toolkit of POSSIBILITIES available to US.

TIPS FOR CHOOSING HABITS

MAKE them SOUND FUN! use words that excite YOU!

MAKE YOUR HABITS FEEL ACHIEVABLE! If it feels OVERWHELMING, KEEP it SIMPLER + MORE DOABLE.

TRACK YOUR habits DAILY to STAY MOTIVATED.

CHOOSE HABITS that help YOU ACHIEVE YOUR BIG GOALS.

ideas for goal getter HABITS

Write 750 words a DAY   Practise Mindfulness

Exercise   Green Smoothie   Single TASK

Process emails ONCE A DAY   Declutter for 10 mins

Eat fresh fruit & veges   Get inbox to Zero

Stick to a 5 sentence Limit on emails

Work while disconnected   Journal dAILy

Make a piece of ART   Declutter Your desk

Follow a Morning Routine   Go for a walk

Read a chapter of A Book   Gratitude journal

Hug A Person or a Pet   Write A thank you Note

Connect with A Friend   Drink 8 glasses of WATER

Write A DAILY to Do List & identify Your 3
M.I.T.s (MOST IMPORTANT TASKS)

Keep A tech-free Bedroom   Practise A Hobby

Practise Self Care   Compliment Someone

Perform a Random ACT OF Kindness

MY goal getter HABITS

MY goals that are so **BIG + DARING** that im not even sure they are **POSSIBLE** are...

what are the **TOP 10** things you want to **DO** in **YOUR Life?**

①
②
③
④
⑤

⑥
⑦
⑧
⑨
⑩

100 things to do!

These can be BIG goals or tiny ones... a culmination of all your goals from this WORKBOOK, or totally NEW ones. Just have FUN & encourage yourself to stretch!

1. _____ ☐
2. _____ ☐
3. _____ ☐
[4.] _____ ☐
5. _____ ☐
6. _____ ☐
7. _____ ☐
8. _____ ☐
9. _____ ☐
10. _____ ☐
11. _____ ☐
12. _____ ☐
13. _____ ☐
14. _____ ☐

15. _____ ☐
16 _____ ☐
17. _____ ☐
18. _____ ☐
19. _____ ☐
20. _____
[21.] _____ ☐
22. _____ ☐
23 _____ ☐
24. _____ ☐
25 _____ ☐
26. _____ ☐
27. _____ ☐
28 _____ ☐

29. _____ □

30. _____ □

31. _____ □

32. _____ □

33. _____ □

34. _____ □

35. _____ □

36. _____ □

37. _____ □

38. _____ □

39. _____ □

40. _____ □

41. _____ □

42. _____ □

43. _____ □

44. _____ □

45. _____ □

46. _____ □

47. _____ □

48. _____ □

49. _____ □

50. _____ □

51. _____ □

52. _____ □

53. _____ □

54. _____ □

55. _____ □

56. _____ □

57. _____ □

58. _____ □

59. _____ □

60. _____ □

61. _____ □

62. _____ □

63. _____ □

64. _____ □

65. _____ □

66. _____ □

67. _____ □

68. _____ □

69. _____ ☐
70. _____ ☐
71. _____ ☐
72. _____ ☐
73. _____ ☐
74. _____ ☐
75. _____ ☐
76. _____ ☐
77. _____ ☐
78. _____ ☐
79. _____ ☐
80. _____ ☐
81. _____ ☐
82. _____ ☐
83. _____ ☐
84. _____ ☐
85. _____ ☐
86. _____ ☐
87. _____ ☐
88. _____ ☐

89. _____ ☐
90. _____ ☐
91. _____ ☐
92. _____ ☐
93. _____ ☐
94. _____ ☐
95. _____ ☐
96. _____ ☐
97. _____ ☐
98. _____ ☐
99. _____ ☐
100. _____ ☐

Dream Big!

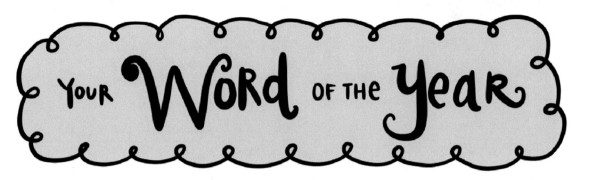

YOUR Word OF THE YeaR

It can Be a DeLiCiOUS PROCeSS to choose a WORD foR YOUR YeaR. THiS can become a Theme, A viSion, an eneRGY foR You to invoke! WRiTe iT iN HeRe ONCe You KNOW it!

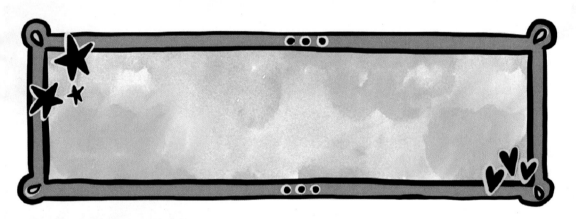

What in YOuR life currently feels like it fits YOUR WORD?	What in Your life currently feels like it DOESN'T fit Your word?

DReaM DaY

I wish this was an Assignment we were given in school.
I wish we'd been taught to DREAM BIG & create the life we want.
At least we are doing it now. It's TIME.
I want you to write in as much Detail as possible
what your DREAM DAY would look like. Where would
you Be? Who would you be with? How would you spend
your time? What would be your Dream WORK?
I promise you, this exercise is powerful. It's time to
become an EXPERT in you + your DREAMS.

Annual Oracle Reading

I began giving myself yearly forecast readings in 2011. It amazed me how accurate + insightful it was as the year unfolded...

ive done it each year since with profound results... & i'd ♥ to invite you to tRY it out for yourself! ☆

♥ HOW To DO YOUR OWN

1. Use whatever holy text or cards feel good to your heart

   Quran   Oracle cards   Poetry book   Sacred book

   Bible   TaROT   Affirmation deck

2. Connect to YOUR peRsonal source of divine guidance

3. Pull a caRd or open to a random page of book foR each Month

4. wRite down the message foR each month that feels most important ♥ ♥!

JANUARY

FEBRUARY

MARCH

APRIL

may

june

july

august

September

October

November

December

DREAMBOARD

DreamBoards are an incredibly powerful tool for visualising what you wish to create. Not only can they be beautiful & inspiring to look at, but they will help you remember every single day your dreams & highest intentions. What you focus on becomes true!

Supplies you will Need ♥

 A piece of cardboard, paper or canvas in the size that feels Right to you

 GLUE

 Scissors

 Magazines, Newspapers, photos + images

add a little blend of Openness, ☆ Courage, JOY + a sprinkle of hope. ♥

Search through MAGAZINES for images + WORDS of things, people, feelings & experiences you'd like to draw into your life for the next year ♥♥♥

Cut out the images that lift you up, inspire you + make you feel RADIANT ♥ Ignore everything that feels like A SHOULD!

ARRANGE on your BOARD until it feels JUST RIGHT to your SPIRIT then GLUE! glue

PLACE it WHERE you can see it DAILY. On YOUR DESK, BY YOUR BED—even on the back of YOUR toilet Door!

You can also use the following page as a DREAMBOARD to keep with YOUR WORKBOOK

You can also use PINTEREST as an online dream BOARD—OR make a digital collage using Canva!

EACH DAY, take ACTIONS that bring YOU CLOSER to YOUR DREAMS

WATCH as YOUR dreams MAGICALLY APPEAR!

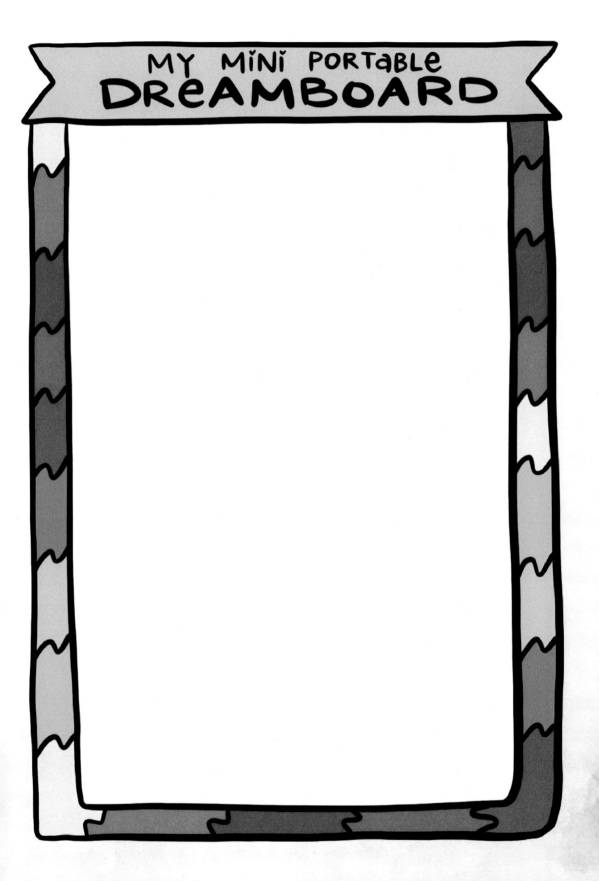

MY MINI PORTABLE
DREAMBOARD

everything you are Looking for is inside

→ YOU ←

How

to make those

beautiful
goals

of yours
come
true!

How To Make Your Goals Happen!

Setting your Goal is just the FIRST step in birthing your dreams into the world.

As you get started in making your Goals happen you may experience feelings like:

This can happen when we see OUR GOAL as just ONE TASK on our to do list.

In REALITY a BIG GOAL like this has MANY indidual tasks to COMPLETE. It looks more like:

You can't
eat a
BURGER
in one bite.

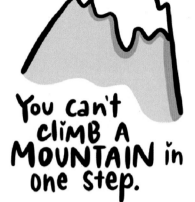

You can't
climb A
MOUNTAIN in
one step.

Goals, mountains + burgers are all the same. They are accomplished one step, one bite, one task at a time.

WHEN IN DOUBT OR PARALYSIS, BREAK THE TASKS DOWN INTO even SMALLER TASKS THAT TAKE LESS than 10 MIN To DO!

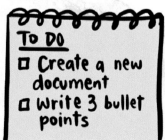

To DO
☐ Create a new document
☐ Write 3 bullet points

MAKING MICRO TASKS LIKE THIS can sometimes really help spur me into Action!
I ♥ ticking things off ☑

☆ Magic Momentum Map

Write Goal Here →

I'd like to have it completed BY:

What DAILY HABITS will help me get there?

Circle What Would Help You:

Co-work Space

Say No to More things

Social MEDIA Sabbatical

Accountability Partner

Coach

RETREAT

Go PUBLIC with YOUR GOAL

How will You CELEBRATE when You Get THERE?

Project Tracker

COLOUR YOUR PROGRESS AS YOU GO! ♥

10% 20% 30% 40% 50% 60% 70% 80% 90%   FINISH!

BREAK YOUR GOAL INTO MICROTASKS!

- [ ]
- [ ]
- [ ]
- [ ]
- [ ]
- [ ]
- [ ]
- [ ]
- [ ]
- [ ]
- [ ]
- [ ]
- [ ]
- [ ]
- [ ]
- [ ]
- [ ]
- [ ]
- [ ]
- [ ]
- [ ]
- [ ]
- [ ]
- [ ]
- [ ]
- [ ]

ADD DEADLINES FOR MICROTASKS!

HIGHLIGHT the most URGENT TASKS

Magic Momentum Map

Write Goal Here ↳

 I'd like to have it Completed BY:

_____

What DAILY HABITS will help me get there?

Circle What Would Help You:

Co-work Space   Say No to More things   Social MEDIA Sabbatical

Accountability Partner   COACH

RETREAT   Go PUBLIC with YOUR GOAL

How will You CELEBRATE when You Get THERE?

Project Tracker

COLOUR YOUR PROGRESS as YOU GO! ♥

10%   20%   30%   40%   50%   60%   70%   80%   90%   FINISH!

BREAK YOUR GOAL INTO MICROTASKS! ♥

☐ _____
☐ _____
☐ _____
☐ _____
☐ _____
☐ _____
☐ _____
☐ _____
☐ _____
☐ _____
☐ _____
☐ _____
☐ _____
☐ _____
☐ _____
☐ _____
☐ _____
☐ _____
☐ _____
☐ _____
☐ _____
☐ _____
☐ _____
☐ _____

☐ _____
☐ _____
☐ _____
☐ _____
☐ _____
☐ _____
☐ _____
☐ _____
☐ _____
☐ _____
☐ _____
☐ _____
☐ _____
☐ _____
☐ _____
☐ _____
☐ _____
☐ _____
☐ _____
☐ _____
☐ _____
☐ _____
☐ _____

ADD DEADLINES FOR MICROTASKS!

HIGHLIGHT the most URGENT TASKS

☆ Magic Momentum Map

Write Goal Here ↳

I'd like to have it completed BY:

_____

What DAILY HABITS will help me get there?

Circle What Would Help You:

Co-work Space

Say No to More things

Social MEDIA Sabbatical

Accountability Partner

Coach

RETREAT

Go PUBLIC with YOUR GOAL

How will you CELEBRATE when you get there?

Project Tracker

COLOUR YOUR PROGRESS as YOU GO! ♥

10%. 20%. 30%. 40%. 50%. 60%. 70%. 80%. 90%.

FINiSH!

BREAK YOUR GOAL INTO MICROTASKS!

- [ ] _____
- [ ] _____
- [ ] _____
- [ ] _____
- [ ] _____
- [ ] _____
- [ ] _____
- [ ] _____
- [ ] _____
- [ ] _____
- [ ] _____
- [ ] _____
- [ ] _____
- [ ] _____
- [ ] _____
- [ ] _____
- [ ] _____
- [ ] _____
- [ ] _____
- [ ] _____
- [ ] _____
- [ ] _____
- [ ] _____

- [ ] _____
- [ ] _____
- [ ] _____
- [ ] _____
- [ ] _____
- [ ] _____
- [ ] _____
- [ ] _____
- [ ] _____
- [ ] _____
- [ ] _____
- [ ] _____
- [ ] _____
- [ ] _____
- [ ] _____
- [ ] _____
- [ ] _____
- [ ] _____
- [ ] _____
- [ ] _____
- [ ] _____
- [ ] _____

ADD DEADLINES FOR MICROTASKS!

HIGHLIGHT the most URGENT TASKS

A **goal** without a **plan** is just a **wish**.

Monthly Checkins

Remember this tasty tidbit from the start of this book?

It's <mark>not enough</mark> to just fill out this WORKBOOK & never look at it again.

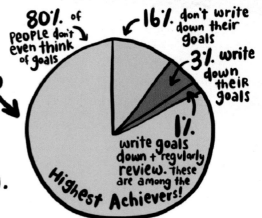

80% of people don't even think of goals

16% don't write down their goals

3% write down their goals

1% write goals down + regularly review. These are among the Highest Achievers!

Highest Achievers!

Remember:

It's the 1% of the population who write down their goals AND regularly review them who are AMONG the → HIGHEST ACHIEVERS ←

And You are going to be one of them. Pull out your calendar now + set a recurring date in your calendar at the start of every month. Come back here, fill out the worksheet & have a monthly date with your dreams ♥♥♥

The Monthly check in sheets will keep you on track, motivated + productive. And you'll join that incredible 1% of people who know how to make their dreams come true!

IT'S TIME TO REVIEW
January!

⭐ What goals did you achieve in Jan?	☑ What goals do you want to have in FEB?
❓ What do you need to do to make them happen?	💕 What self care do you wish to feel in FEB?

IT'S TIME TO REVIEW

February

☆ What goals did you achieve in FeB?	☑ What goals do you want to have in March?

❓ What do you need to do to make them happen?	🖤 What self care do you wish to feel in MARCH?

IT'S TIME TO REVIEW

March

⭐ **What goals did you achieve in March?**	☑ **What goals do you want to have in APRIL?**
❓ **What do you need to do to make them happen?**	💛 **What self care do you wish to feel in April?**

IT'S TIME TO REVIEW

APRIL

⭐ What goals did you achieve in APRIL?	☑ What goals do you want to have in MAY?

❓ What do you need to do to make them happen?	💗 What self care do you wish to feel in May?

IT'S TIME TO REVIEW

MAY

⭐ What goals did you achieve in May?	☑ What goals do you want to have in June?

❓ What do you need to do to make them happen?	💗 What self care do you wish to feel in June?

IT'S TIME TO REVIEW
JUNE

☆ **What goals did you achieve in June?**

☑ **What goals do you want to have in JULY?**

❓ **What do you need to do to make them happen?**

💗 **What self care do you wish to feel in JULY?**

IT'S TIME TO REVIEW

* JULY *

☆ What goals did you achieve in July?	☑ What goals do you want to have in August?

? What do you need to do to make them happen?	♥ What self care do you wish to feel in August?

IT'S TIME TO REVIEW
AUGUST

⭐ **What goals did you achieve in August?**

☑ **What goals do you want to have in Sept?**

❓ **What do you need to do to make them happen?**

❤ **What self care do you wish to feel in Sept?**

IT'S TIME TO REVIEW

September

⭐ **What goals did you achieve in September?**	☑ **What goals do you want to have in Oct?**
❓ **What do you need to do to make them happen?**	🖤 **What self care do you wish to feel in Oct?**

IT'S TIME TO REVIEW

OCTOBER

⭐ What goals did you achieve in OCTOBER?	☑ What goals do you want to have in Nov?

❓ What do you need to do to make them happen?	💙 What self care do you wish to feel in Nov?

IT'S TIME TO REVIEW
♥ NOVEMBER ♥

☆ What goals did you achieve in November?	☑ What goals do you want to have in Dec?

❓ What do you need to do to make them happen?	💗 What self care do you wish to feel in Dec?

IT'S TIME TO REVIEW

♥ DECEMBER ♥

☆ What goals did you achieve in December?	☑ What goals do you want to have in JAN?

❓ What do you need to do to make them happen?	♥ What self care do you wish to feel in JAN?

★ TIME TO GET YOUR NEXT WORKBOOKS!

what to do when you FALL OFF the Goal Getter wagon!

①. FORGIVE YOURSELF! SOMETIMES WE GET BUSY. SOMETIMES WE FORGET. IT IS NATURAL + NORMAL TO BE HUMAN + MAKE MISTAKES!

⬇

②. REVIEW YOUR GOALS. READ THROUGH THIS WORKBOOK AGAIN. WHAT GOALS COULD YOU ACHIEVE THIS MONTH?

⬇

③. Go PUBLIC. TELL A FRIEND OR ACCOUNTABILITY BUDDY YOUR GOAL. ASK THEM TO HOLD YOU ACCOUNTABLE.

⬇

④. Go Get YOUR GOAL! REMEMBER THAT MOMENTUM BUILDS MOMENTUM. EVERY LITTLE WIN BREEDS MORE WINS. YOU'VE GOT THIS! KEEP GOING!

 DON'T FOCUS ON WHAT I'M UP

against.

FOCUS ON MY GOALS + try to ignore tHE

 rest. — VENUS WILLIAMS

About the Author:

Leonie Dawson is a best-selling author and serial entrepreneur. Over the past 20 years she has taught hundreds of thousands of gorgeous humans how to build wildly abundant businesses and embrace their creative gifts.

Leonie has been recognised for her business acumen as winner of Ausmumpreneur's Global Brand Award, Businesses Making A Difference Award & People's Choice Business Coach.

WEBSITE: www.LeonieDawson.com
PODCAST: Leonie Dawson Refuses To Be Categorised
ACADEMY: LeonieDawson.com/Academy

YOUR Next STEPS

→

4 weeks behind-the-scenes e-course on how
I've built a multi-million dollar net worth

ARE YOU READY to EARN MORE, teach MORE & finally Get YOUR e-course done?

Are you still messing about NOT getting your e-course done? Or are you not sure how to use the tech behind it? Or have you created an e-course but it's not getting the sales you want from it?

In the span of 40 days, you are going to get your e-course DONE. And master the tech like a pro. And start SELLING it like crazy.

This is accountability, tech + marketing advice on SPEED.

LEONIEDAWSON.COM/ECOURSE

It's time to STOP talking ABOUt writing A Book... & FINISHING → it iN 40 DAYS insteAD...

Want to get your book written, finished and out in the world, doing what it's supposed to be doing?

★ helping the people it is meant to
★ giving you expert status
★ bringing you new clients & customers
★ giving you an extra income stream?

Learn the book writing + book marketing success secrets from and internationally best-selling author who has sold over a million dollars in books!

LEONIEDAWSON.COM/BOOK

Want to know exactly How to sell MORE (OR ANY!) of your thing?

Consider this program an essential business success building block. In order to succeed in business you MUST learn how to sell, and do it well.

Sales Star is my much-requested long-awaited sales training.

- ★ The sales checklists & templates I use in my own business
- ★ Behind the scenes in selling over $14m in 10 hours a week
- ★ Create powerful, magnetic sales pages that make you MORE $$$
- ★ Things to fix to INSTANTLY to start earning more.

Essential for new + mature business owners alike.

LEONIEDAWSON.COM/SELL

You **CAN** grow A PROSPEROUS, PRofitaBLe Biz without SociAL MeDiA!

When people find out I took a two year sabbatical from social media & still made over $2 million in revenue, they immediately say: "Can you even DO that? I want to do that. But, I don't feel like I can."

This workshop gives you:

- ★ 150+ ways to market your business without social media
- ★ 42 reasons to consider leaving social media
- ★ Successful case studies of businesses who don't use social media
- ★ How to increase your profit & reduce your work hours if you do decide to stay on social media.

LEONiE DAWSON. COM/MARKETING

Are you ready to grow a beautifully abundant business & shining life? Join 5,000+ gorgeous humans in my Brilliant Biz & Life Academy!

- ★ Dozens of my incredibly powerful, popular programs
- ★ Group coaching & monthly guest experts
- ★ Done-for-you templates, resources & checklists!

Get everything you need to grow A shining life & Biz ... all at a WILDLY AFFORDABLE price!

LEONIEDAWSON.COM/ACADEMY

Made in United States
Orlando, FL
30 December 2024

56715956R00088